The last of the lig

*for my son, Matthew*

Everything changes, nothing dies.

Ovid

### *Keepsakes*

*Your smile –*
*Put it in this box*
*So that I can take it out*
*And look at it*
*Whenever I need to.*

*Your loud laugh –*
*Decorate it with beads*
*Place it on a branch*
*Outside the window*
*It will sing*
*When the wind blows.*

*Those pinpoint bright stars*
*That lit your eyes*
*With their warm fires –*
*Press them gently back*
*Into the teddybear face of the sky*
*I'll feel their light*
*In the darkest midnight.*

*Your big hands –*
*That clasped my shoulders sometimes*
*That held your own boy close*
*Changed his nappy*
*Fed him his dinner*
*Held his hand to keep him safe*

*Your strong hands –*
*That gripped the paddle*
*That time we went down the river*

*That were raised to shield your eyes*
*As you gazed off into the hazy distance*
*The last time I saw you*

*That sometimes must have pressed down hard*
*Over your own face*
*Trying to keep everything*
*Out and in*

*Your generous hands –*
*That were always open*
*Like your heart*
*To everything and everyone*

*Let's stitch them*
*Into a pair of magic gloves*
*So that I can slip my own hands into them*
*And maybe the cold*
*Won't bite so hard.*

# Contents

# The last of the light is not the last of the light

David Calcutt

**morning light off the estuary**

morning light off the estuary   an unfolding silk

a curlew's cry trembles
in the grass of the mudflats
delicate as falling hair
and ripples across the wide flat water
where edges are melting
and a stillness holds like a raised hand
and a voice says

            *wait*
*wait for the moment*
*it will come*

and all is dissolving   all is being gathered
into the skirts of milky light
that is the one prayer that was not uttered
and standing here inside the stillness
is the one rite that was not performed

it is in the stillness
it is in the waiting
it is in the moment of
stillness and waiting

for the hand to be dipped   cupped   raised
for the spilled golden water   brimming over

### Tree Sings the Blackbird

Flings the chirp and rattle out, the long-trilled
stutter of dappled song, that spills
a rippled, glistening stream, a dreamwork

weave of linked and golden light into the day's
bright gleam, where it catches fire, a flash
of startled flame, a streaking rush of shout

and sheeted lightning, slick across the fencetop
to strut, a burning berry
in its beak.
                   But all's not glance and fire

for here, inside the ivy's attic
dark, there's shadow-black, a warm
of hush and rustle, of mutterings

and secret whisperings, conspiracies
and hatched plans, and a twiggy tangle
of fingered strings, where tree

sings another music, of eggs
like moons in the starry root, and the tap
and the tap of the knuckle on the shell

and the midnight bell, that rings
like a bird, and starts awake
the goblin eyeblink staring out.

## The Sisters' Lament

The trees are weeping  fat drops drip
from the leaves   plop soundless in the mist
that deadens the footfall    the face veiled   weeping

birdsong    madsong   shriek of mourning women
hair loose hanging from the wet branches    their nails
tear their faces    the cracked bark where the nuthatch

is searching   here? where?  in here?  o where?
and the woodpecker laughs   there  over there
and claps and he's off  to leave the twigs trembling

grappling the air   scrabbling in freefall   stooping
to search the smoking wreckage    for the smashed
body   brother's bones in the ground lodged among

roots   to which they are rooted   that clutch
and hold fast   locked and lost  ghosts in the
misty air   searching   frozen   weeping   silent

# Three Visions of the Blast Furnace

## 1  their backs are bent

their backs are bent over rivers of flame   slow-flowing
streams of molten metal bearing away
the souls of the damned    masked with steel visors
clamped down over the bone   as if they are warriors
forged from these flames   where the dead are calling
with machine-screech voices   tongues riveted
to their own cries   the vast halls that rise about them
restless   with shadow and red light   as they are restless
in their labour   feeding the furnaces   all humanity
stripped   seared   burned away   leaving only the endless
effort of toil   the ingrained smell   of sweat and oil
the infernal grins   flame-fixed on their faces

## 2  He is a rider

He is a rider in a chariot taking the long way home.

A step up from the stop
an easy swing round the grasped pole.
The bell rings.

*Move along please.*

Always the same place,
left-hand side near the front,
outer seat, so that others have to push by.

*I never saw him stand.*

And the cap pulled down across his brow
and the canvas bag across his lap
and the newspaper folded in his pocket.

*Standing room only downstairs.*

The oil streaked face,
the grime of heat.
Reek of stale sweat
and burned flesh.

*Fares please.*

He presses his coin
to the proffered palm
takes his ticket.
The payment's made.

*I never heard him speak.*

He puts up with it, tight-lipped.
Takes out his newspaper,
keeps his mouth shut.

*Hold on tight.*

As the bus shudders into a lower gear
and begins its long slow climb uphill.

### 3  I was standing on the hilltop

I was standing on a hilltop above the town,
hand pressed into my father's, looking down
as the blast-furnaces opened their great doors
and a tidal wave of red flame poured

upward into the molten night
so that I could almost feel its surge of heat
like a burning veil against my face, and it seemed
that from that crucible of holy flame

a smouldering angel wreathed in smoke
arose, wings spread and jewelled with sparks,
and stood there in the sky.  Its shadow fell
across the wounded streets as if to heal,

as it rose higher still above the town
and became a blood-red moon.
The vision faded and was gone,
and on the darkening hill I stood alone.

### The Sword in the Stone

*Who grasps me grasps*

the iron in the fire, the flame
in the forge   burning burning
the heart of the heat, the heat
in the heart of stone that sings
and rings with its metal.

*Who grasps me grasps*

the hand with its hammer
the hiss and the sputter of sparks
in the dark, the holy candle
burning burning   anointing
the brow of the wizard who bends
his breath to the bellows
who conjures a king.

*Who grasps me grasps*

the beaten blade, its edge
of rainbows, flowering a crown
of fire, of thorns, the wheel
spinning that cracks at its centre, splits
stone, splits atom, a bloom
of glory   burning burning
the shining city   burning
Burning.

## Dark Journey

I came a long way to find you

across the snow-ridged top with its black gash of road,
its single tree, its burden of sky
and the figures buried deep in the ice.

Now I'm waiting at the station but where are you?

Your train has left early,
or perhaps it's never going to arrive,

travelling somewhere in a no-man's-land
where the shutters of mist have come down across the windows
and nothing exists but your breath on the glass,

your face peering through with all its bones showing.

You have forgotten who I am,
I am forgetting who you are.

As the rails draw likes wires from the back of my skull
and run out through my eyes, emptying them
into your incalculable distance,

the unguessed-at-never-dreamed-of-destination –

a village of broken dolls' houses
where the snow falls like ash
and all voices are frozen like the keys in the lock

of the door you want to open onto that other landscape,

the one where two strangers meet
and exchange names and numbers
and amongst all the rubbish of the fallen towns

a sudden, unexpected flower blooms.

## That Day of Leaving

That day of leaving
there was a mist
over the hills and on the sea

it was like a shutter
pulled down across the brain.
A kestrel hung

below the cloud
it was seeking the rabbit
that sat cowering

in my skull. You, curlew
were nowhere to be seen
your cry lay sodden

on the muddy shore
a length of frayed rope
coiled beneath dunes

and the boat
that moored there
set adrift,

its only passenger
my homeless ghost.
Sing, curlew,

lead me to a landing.

# LUD

## I

Deep cleft cut
through the head's green world,

exposing roots, ancient tracks,
the petrified, migratory
flightpaths of birds

and a slow, hidden breathing,
the secret word cradled
in cupped hands,

kept close, as a fire in its hearth,
a blade in its sheath,

the eye, ever watchful
in its hidden chamber.

## II

We came first to the high place
where creatures of rock
straddled their kingdom,

cumbersome, reptilian,
wreathed in their own smoky breath.
Their roar was the wind

that took the skin from our faces.
Then we travelled the spiny ridge-back,
happy explorers of that early world

with our sandwiches and teaflasks
armour against the strangeness
and the big wings of brightness

and the hollow ground
that echoed beneath our feet
and the voice that spoke from far off

calling us down.

## III

The knight kneeling in his armour –
a lonely stone on the hill slope.

The lord feasting in his castle –
a fox snuffling at the bones of a sheep.

The lady sewing in her chamber –
a hawk hanging to the threads of the wind.

And, deep within the folds
of the labyrinth rock,
humped like a crow over its carrion,

the storyteller makes this tale,
sharp as the moon's edge,
bloody as a sunset,

from the breath of his god
that gives each word its bite.

**IV**

Man of mossy stone

frayed trousers,
mildewed, muddy jacket
and feet grown down

into the ground.

After long wandering you've found your resting place

at home with the woodlice
and in the earthworm's gut

where the lizard peers
from its crevice lookout,

happy to ease yourself
out of your bones,
let wind and weather pick you apart,

become mush of earth, log-mash,
root-drip, frond-glimmer

and this slow, soft breathing
among the silky, green draperies

as she lays you down
for a last kiss,

her true love,

the one we've come looking for.

## Sunrise on Midsummer Morning

A full moon falling, the sky lit
with last night's charred and crumbling embers

across the field, thin spills of misty light

visiting spirits haunt the hedges
or try a cry in the canal's bandaged ear

dung reeks and steams, a horse's hoof strikes home

and out of the trees the great bird rises
wings spread and beating the sky into flame

and the great egg of the world is hatched

with an outflung shout and tumble of voices
many and many, song of all songs.

*

Later on oak's shoulder
an owl puts on a mask of light

and the big mothers with their babies
stand among thistles and stare.

**Lord of the Wood**

Today I saw the lord of the wood,
stepping out daintily the paths of his realm
and he was branched with glory, and crowned
with the morning and the dripping light.

He was shadow and he was leaf-shade,
he was the riven heart of the oak tree
whose roots sang themselves through his blood
and he was nameless in his kingdom.

Custom was strong in him, the secrets
of that neighbourhood were velvet
to his ears. The balance of the year
was weighed between his shoulder blades.

Today I saw the lord of the wood,
I came upon him unawares as his gaze
struck my moment. And I would weep
for the knowing that was put into my heart.

**She is trying to get back to what she was**

She is howling a loneliness

it is the shriek of the polar wind across blasted spaces
it is the deep-under-ice lamenting of whales
the throat-cry of seals, shadows in a blizzard

she is howling a loneliness.

She is folding the ocean into her body

it lifts a great hump it shoulders the sky
it glitters with creatures their frozen voices
then cracks and splits and falls back empty

she is folding the ocean into her body.

She is dreaming a dark dream

a man in crows' feathers a man with a drum
he carries a bag it is filled with songs
he carries a spear his talk is crooked

she is dreaming a dark dream.

She is combing her hair into the sky

she pulls at the knots they bleed a sunset
it is filled with stars and the northern lights
its nuclear glow spreads across the world

she is combing her hair into the sky.

She is eating her father

his skin is the flag of his last kingdom
she is stitching his ghost into the emptiness
the needles she uses are made of his bones


she is eating her father.

She is trying to get back to what she was.

## Hector Dragged around Troy

With heels tied to the back of Achilles' chariot dead
eyes staring in horror at his own death escaping
from between his teeth naked his body torn into raw
rags of flapping flesh trampled by the hooves of the
horses whose terrified screaming rips out over the raw
wounds of their tongues and it's all thunder and storm
and dust and heat under a wide blind sky and there's
his soul looking on aghast in the moments before it's
dragged away itself to become a twittering insect
in the nowhere world and Achilles meanwhile leaps
from his chariot leaving the horses still racing the
body bouncing along behind and runs with his grief
still bloodspattered and raw into the camp to kneel
in the dirt and kiss the lips of his dead lover.

## Broken Children

I went looking for them
in the empty room
where the sad music was playing

and a woman's voice was singing
of the deaths of children.

There's a single window
hung with cobwebs
where half sketched faces
look in through the glass,

seeking their childhoods,
those lost toys.

They find them laid out on a table
neatly arranged –
hands, feet, heads, mouths,
the folded skin suits

but the smiles are left out.

In another room a child is laughing.
Here there's no such sound.
Your brother is painting his night world,
your sister is sleeping in his cold bed.

You stare at each other
across these polished spaces
with eyes that bore through
to the back of the skull.

What is it you're whispering?
What secrets are shared?
What night fear flutters behind the mask?
What fury flaps its wings at your back?

Your mothers and fathers don't know what they do.

But when the lights are switched off
and the bedroom door's locked
and nobody's watching
you can come out to play.

Set the silver top humming,
tell the scary tale.

## DIG

**I**

And we are on our knees
faces close to the ground
with earthworms

and the ends of roots
scraping at stones, the broken
bones of words

listening for voices
to come clear of the dirt
speak a new language

chopped syllables of light.

## II

The river is nearby

a tree bending over the river
wind in its leaves

folding them back
with its careful fingers

to show a sky
on which nothing is written

only air and light
and an open space

like hands cupped
for a gift

where a soft rain falls.

**III**

The tree is twisting itself
into a man

the man is trying
to twist himself
into a tree.

Each is straining to become
what it is not.

It's an agony in the garden

where the wren
proclaims its outcry
water falls

drop by drop
into the hollow stone bowl.

**IV**

You try to speak
what cannot be spoken.
The silence sticks in your throat
a rusty pin.

Then – you listen

to the ticking of the clock
the lifting of the latch
the dull tap and clink
of metal on stone

to the sunlight that falls
onto old ground
and spills over its edges

as the river in flood
overspills its bank

smoothing the wounds
made by words
the deep trench cut
by the tongue's blade.

## V

Who inhabits this space

where no foot treads
where the foot that does tread

leaves no print?

Whose voice is speaking
within the silence?

What kindly spirit
waits in the silence

to take the top off your skull
and empty it of everything?

**VI**

Sudden glare – up off the river
wingbeat of flame – from out of the leaves.

A cry of joy
or terror.

That mossy stone you hold in your hands –

isn't that just your own head
with the face worn smooth
and the eyes staring blankly
into unguessable distances

a hair's breadth behind the lids?

Roots are curling out of its mouth
a moth crawls out of its ear

and way up there a first star blinks
in the dark of your blood
holds its breath

listening.

## VII

Lift it from the earth
feel its rough, pitted surface
its broken edge

a weight in your hand.
It's all you have left.

That, and the moment by moment unravelling
of tree into sky
day into dusk

and the hard earth packed under your knee.

A woman's shadow crosses the grass.
A lifted finger is pressed to your lips.

Look up
see the archway of a last light

letting fall its shadow
a crumbling of dust.

**VIII**

The walls are tumbling back into their pits.

The church has flown off into the air.

Everywhere, a kind of apocalypse.

Even that skylark above the field
is unpicking each stitch of the light
with its voice.

Now, when there is nothing left to salvage
And everything has been washed clean of its name

dig.

# Mouth Bow

**I**

You place the tip across your mouth

hold it still, the shaped beechwood
sliver of a new moon's edge in your hand.

Between your fingers
the flat oval of bone.

A touch, resting. Then – pluck the strung gut.

\*\*\*

It sings in his head.
Twang. Then
a deep honeywarm drone
struck through his whole shattered being

as if his soul is speaking to itself
of a creature sleeping in a cave of bone

dreaming it is a man
who dreams he is not.

\*\*\*

Meanwhile the mouth moves

like an animal trying to escape its trap
writhing a grimace of articulation
through the slowly woven web of harmonics
the delicate strings of tangled sound

that hold it fast as it struggles to break free

to flee the snare
to speak its song.

**II**

Let the eye sharpen

let the gaze narrow along a smoothed shaft
to the chiselled point

let alignment pause as the lips purse
their one, pure note
eased out
in a slow unfolding ripple of air
the surefire slipstream of the bright blade of sound.

Dead
shot.

Let the song free
let the arrow fly

\*\*\*

Drumming in the hooves of the herds on the grassland.

\*\*\*

That leap across this cave wall to the music of arrows

where the figure dances to the thumb-struck string
to the ghost-song breathed through the flute of bone.

That gives my breath its word
its bright blade.

\*\*\*

O poetry

O bloody song of the hunter.

### A pale sun rising

a blind sky
fog over frosted fields
ghost of a sun
come to mourn
its own passing
face cracked
with the black
silhouette of trees
mere sketches
a charcoal afterthought

whose birds
have no songs
to fashion a landscape
no word to utter
of world's making
only a

silence
draped like a veil
a white shroud laid
across the fields
whose edges burn
with a sullen fire
a last flame, the light

of the world.

## End of september

**1**

little brace-
bridge pool where
dimpled wrinkles on the water
are insects taptoeing
a fish kissing
the smooth surface otherwise
stilled some
hand's held mirror
where you can see
sky trees clouds yourself
the eye's untampered circle
and sink into it

**2**

then the horses
come down
step out of the trees
you might think
on two legs at first
but then four
five of them
wild ponies to drink
and swish their shaggy tails
blackmaned nibbling
manifest of their habitat
a man kneels
and photographs snaps
the harness ring of the lens
he thinks
he's caught them

**3**

you hear them first
the two buzzards
longdistance shot
wheeling screaming above
the treetops
lakota ghost-
dancers in
their fringed shirts
stepshuffling the air calling
on manitou
they make a sun
with their wings' circle
then vanish back
into the black hills

**4**

at the bigger brace-
bridge pool
(after a short walk
through woods along tracks
of lightmottled grass-shadow
bulk-rustle in the under-
growth) the long-
tailed tits skim
themselves across the surface
with bounce and chuckle
and delight at all things
made here and now
and visible and now
flipped coins out of
heaven's purse
they too come to play.

## Sheep

On a bank above
the sea white
cliffs no fences

her coarse
thick coat heavy
with her smell

and the smell
of warm earth
eden perhaps

before man waked
a wind
stirs the grass

finger of some
god of beasts
spilling light

across her back
her lit head
raised fearless

dry bleat
over a hard
tongue calling

others up out
of the foam
of the sea.

## Aten

**I**

Risen song
a pure, clear note
struck from skyline to skyline
across the hedgetops

the night's burst wrappings
consumed in flame.

Warrior of the morning
traversing the earth,
you drag the world to waking in your flarepath.

The fields are your armies,
they send up a clamour of joy as you pass.
The sun flies your banner,
a bright scattering,

and light flashes from the blades of many weapons.

## II

With the sun hammered mast-high
between the spread sails of your wings,

with the twisted ropes of the wind taut
to hold you in balance,

with the compass point fixed
to its only star,

you hang the hook of your gaze
between the horizons,
hold the world stilled,

the motorway embankment,
the leathery trees,
the clockwork heartbeat of the mouse
stilled

but for this quivering of wingtips

poised at the zenith
on the blade's tip
before the long slide down,

the nirvana of drop.

## III

You perch in the rafters
of your cathedral of evening,
feet gripped to the one remaining wire of light

slowly loosening itself from the sun,

The rest drifts and crumbles
across the wide floors of the meadows.

You are listening to the last sounds you will ever hear,

becoming a hieroglyph on the wall of your own tomb,
its treasure scattered among the scavengers.

They have taken it down to the lower world.
You are following to find it,
folding the map of the land in your feathers,

that ancient parchment, your happy hunting grounds.

You will be gone a long time.
When will you return
with your wings' timbrel,

your risen song.

**The wren came to me in a dark dream**

*The wren came to me*
*in a dark dream*

it tapped on the window
I wouldn't let it in

it sat on the windowsill
it sang bright needles

> *they sewed my eyelids*
> *they pierced my tongue.*

*The wren came to me*
*in a dark dream*

it pecked a hole in my skull
it filled it with spiders

it wore a nightmare mask
I hid in the wardrobe

> *in the deep of the cave*
> *the rag-man shivering.*

*The wren came to me*
*in a dark dream*

it perched on my shoulder
I drank hot blood

it buzzed in my ear
I fantasized murders

> *a thorn in the heart*
> *a christ in its coffin.*

*The wren came to me*
*in a dark dream*

it flapped bony wings
it spoke love it spoke weeping

it told me its secret
I stared in the mirror

      *it showed me a stranger*
I couldn't move
        *it showed me a ghost*
I never moved again.

# TATTERCOATS

## A Coat of Nettles

I put on a coat of nettles. Oh!
they burned, they turned me inside
out with their scratchy fingernails.

My skin became another animal
it went prowling through the streets
of pain, wherever it trod

there was dereliction.
I danced the dance of a man
in flames, the saint of nowhere.

I became ancient but not wise.
I crawled into the broken place
where my toys lay strangled

and sat holding my hurt
like a heart torn out
that goes on beating

so that even my mother's ghost
could bring no comfort.
Far off I heard my skin howling.

## A Coat of Cobwebs

Somebody was looking at me
from out of the cubbyhole
under the stairs. Dead eye.
Dead mouth. A doll's head maybe.

The eye blinked. The mouth
puckered into a smile. *Come in*
she said. I crept into this fairytale.
It was an old woman hunched

over her spinning wheel. Clack.
Clack. Bent back, arthritic fingers
and a face like a mask
of dirty secrets. But the song

she sang was sweet poison
a lullaby hypodermic. I rocked
in the cradle of her hunger.
When I woke I was wearing

a coat of cobwebs, an old man
in an armchair gathering dust
with all her children gathered
to hear my story.

## A Coat of Rags

I went looking for a coat of rags
naked, glossy raw. The moonlight
burned me, the night set its dogs loose

to snap at my heels.  Somehow
I escaped them and took refuge
under a tree of curses.  I listened

to the wind muttering its nothings
and sat and prayed to the whatever god
like someone stripped down

to his heart's bone.  An outlaw gang
of rascals found me, gathered me up
out of the fallen leaves

with their clever fingers put the pieces
back together.  They fitted a rat's mask
over my face, gave me a coat

made of the rags of their crimes.
Glass buttons for eyes, a mouth
stitched with black laughter.

Now I chatter witchcraft, read the future
in nutshells, dig my mother's bones
from the frozen earth.

## A Coat of Stars

I saw this star shining
it was trapped in a raindrop.
I slid towards it sticky-
smooth. A tonguelash

of white fire emptied
me out. Someone breathed
and I bulbed like a fat thumb
pressing my print

into the maker's face.
I chomped leaf, sucked
mulch, I reared up dragon-
like to devour the moon.

Then the night opened
its book of wonders
the rain wrapped me
in a coat of stars.

I made love with myself
and we became thousands.
We left behind us a trail
of broken jewels.

# A Coat of Water

I found this coat of water
soft, slimy smooth, almost the colour
of nobody. I slipped it on, it slipped
off again. I went diving in for it

among the weedy relics.
Goggle-eyes gaped, friendly monsters
massaged each other with their jaws.
I wriggled deeper into the mud

of my ancestors.  My arms, my legs
fell away, my face drifted loose
I became just this mouth
in a jungle of beginnings

I ate everybody I had ever known.
Their ghosts became a coat of water
smooth, slimy soft, almost a disappearing
colour. I slipped it on, it slipped

off again, I melted into the ooze
of everywhere, I was just this black speck
in the corner of an eyeblink.
Somebody wept me out in a tear.

## A Coat of Roots

I put on a coat of feathers.  I cried
I wanted to fly, I wanted to rise
up and kiss the sun, but the feathers

held me down, a weight of chains
about my neck, my feet stuck
fast in the branch they clung to.

Bark knotted itself about me, it sat
me squat in a labyrinth of leaves
staring out at the smokedrift

of the crumbling world. A shutter
came down, my gaze ricocheted
inward.  I heard the shuffling

of the underworld, smelled sap
touched spore, the fibrous dark
wrapped me in a coat of roots.

I lost myself. I became a mingling
of everything, kindly tendrils
of fungus picked me apart.

There was a green silence
the warm stillness of woods.
No more hurt. I rested.

## Hob Jack

The rat's in the water
                    old Hob Jack
the devil of a creature.  Hair-twitch-nose-tip
an inch above the surface, grinning
what games to play in the garden

where blowflies hum
and midges strum
the new dawn's daystrings.
                    Hark! What's that?
A moorchick clacks among the reeds,
the Rush Queen's daughter, come to gather
the scattered petals of morning.
                    Jack blinks
Jack sinks
to the darkest room in the murky gloom
for dirty deeds. Offstage laughter.
                    Old Hob
's on the job
planning bloody murder.  It's in his nature,
his joy's in the frenzy and flood of the kill
and the calm that comes after.
                    Snick snack
the mirror cracks,
a tumble and flurry and someone goes down
to be lost forever.
                    The pool closes over.

Someone calls.


                    But who can find
the Rush Queen's daughter? And who will mourn
for her feathered crown broken on the water?
The pool stills. The sky's dry-eyed.
                    And where's
Hob Jack?
He's gone underground. He's biding his time,

58

he's adding another crime to his book
of robbery and slaughter. And his new bride
sits on her underworld throne, far from any sun,
grown terrible, grown strong.
                                    She's forgotten
her mother.
And out in the reed-beds a ghost bird shrieks.
          Hob Jack's
on the run.
And the day's just begun.

Now that tale's done.

## GRACE

After the catastrophe
you planted a seed
among the ruins
watered it with a last tear.

It grew into a world of many wonders

in which I woke
from my coma
to the heart's stillness
the sun's silence

your absence.

\*

Your wild dog
was a carrying a message.

I set off to track it down
in and out of fretful sleep
emptied of everything
but my obsession

that line of dark tracks
printed in the dust.

The careful stitching
in my skin came loose
where I walked, nothing
had begun to live.

When finally I caught up with it
I had blood on my hands.

I sat, cradling its head in my arms
as first one star died, and then another.

From far off I heard you calling.

*

I made a flute of bone
its making outlasted
many loves, many lifetimes.

I went beyond the edge
of the great emptiness
when I came back
I was someone else.

But there it was
in my hands
a simple, cheery thing.

I was going to summon you
back from the dead land.

I put my mouth to its lips
I breathed out.

Beyond the flames' reach
something shuffled closer.

*

The jackals have come for me.
I travel with them
to the secret graveyard
at the far edge.

They keep watch as I sit
talking to the dead
trying to help them
free themselves of death.

But the dead don't listen
they're busy with
something else.
And already the sun

is beginning to rise
dawn's cracking
its knuckles
the jackals are hungry.

\*

The way leads to a wood

trees like oily smoke
fingers groping, knotted in prayer.

Faces among the trees
a gibbering of tongues.

I cut my way through

they cry out, they weep
I show no mercy.

I cut, they cry out
the agony is endless.

But somewhere
beyond this nightmare

is beauty, a smile.

*

I pulled you from the wreckage
of the meteorite that crashed into earth.

Dead or alive, I couldn't tell
there was little difference.

Now I can't put you down
I have to carry you with me

as I travel across the borders
through the empty towns

the shadows of other people
bearing the weight

of your annihilation.
And with each step

your pain grows heavier
you become lighter

I become you.

\*

My friend was sitting
among flakes of falling autumn leaves

he was looking at his hands
that were no longer there

he began to laugh
through the gash of his mouth.

I sat with him
as at a hospital bedside

in that interminable silence
when there's nothing left to say

and it's time to leave.
And this was not hell

it was not even purgatory
or a life-sentence.

This was just one of the many rooms
in the palace of love.

*

I was walking through fire.
There was no pain
an intense heat, perhaps
that wrapped me in its wings

and a brightness that sang.

Others too were moving beside me
shadows, spirits.
Some I thought I knew
or remembered from other times.

But nowhere among them
was the one I looked for.
You were elsewhere
beyond the flames' reach

this endless striving
for salvation. This bitter

waking to a cold dawn.

*

I woke on some beach or other.
I didn't know how I'd come there.

A flat sea, strange light on the water

and this high-pitched
insect-humming in my ear.

The weight of a mountain
was lumped in my chest.

I was like a man at the end of a long trek
some vital part left behind.

Then, far off, a figure walking towards me.

The sea brightened
the horizon darkened.

Always the same dream
and it's never you.

*

One by one
those masks fall away
this one, that one

the painted devil
the weeping sinner
the sainted mask

of righteous suffering.
I cast them
like dead skins

they fall away
and lie crumpled
on the ground.

The wind scatters them
a whispering
of cold ashes.

I have no need of them.
All I need is here.
My outstretched hands

printed with your face.

*

I looked up and saw
the radiance of heaven

it was revealed to me just
in the instant of forgetting.

You were there too, though
your face was turned away

a pinpoint of light receding
to zero. It was your gift to me

a last offering. Then I was
back here where you

were not. My friends smiled
and asked me how I was.

I didn't answer. My tongue
couldn't move. I could

not move. My feet were
fast in ice. I saw a star

fall to earth.

*

I only saw you for a moment
you didn't see me at all
then I lost you in the crowd
just moments before
the bomb went off.

Later, in the afterlife
you became a tree
and I was a bird, hidden
among your branches
your stillness, my restlessness

your silence my song.

***

## Absence of the White Heron

I came along the path that led towards the water

and there, at the bend near the top of the slope
was the water. A clear view across,
like a half-waking dream of water

where a fish composed entirely of light
darted and dropped again
to the underbelly dark

and there were silences nesting
among the stiff grasses,
there was held breath, a web's trembling,
an eye not blinking.

And that stillness –
a flat slab of stone too heavy for me to lift.

But someone was making something wonderful
down there in the marsh-bed, and I stood,
waiting for it to appear,

stepping out from the reeds,
dark-eyed, my spirit-bird,

unfolding itself with each tread
of its foot, wings spread
for the longed-for lift

and flight.  Then,

a flurry of wind-glitter off the wet trees
that flashed and spattered
across the broken surface

and the miracle was gone before it had chance to happen,
the hand drew back and closed on its gift.

There was birdsong in the woods,
the raucous outcries of crows,
the ordinary morning shrugged itself awake.

I turned from the path.
It began to snow.

## The Grief Tree

Winter. The worst time.  Dark of the year.
The cold biting deep. Riven spirit, the
bone-crunching season.

I was stumbling in a wood, shade
among shadows, a tangle of pathless
hanging branches –
                                        lost
among the suicides, perhaps,
each creak of branch a cracked life speaking –
          *who is it where are you is it you?*
Dead leaf whisper under the skin.

I took my need to a tree –
                                        an oak
as it happens, wreathed with ivy –
pressed my brow, gripped my hand,
held on while the tree drew me inward
and drove my grief like a spike through its hard bark
screaming at the centre.

Seeking a shriving.
                    The prayer descended

to where root-tip met mineral
and a fat seed lay curled
in its comfy bed.
No heartbeat, but a slow pulse,
          *du-dum du-dum*
an old ache ripening.

And this was where I wanted to be this
was what I wanted
                          to be.
But was not.

A cry called me back. Something
came free. The invisible blackbird
spoke close up –
                          *time to be going time to be gone.*

A chip of bark on my forehead.
I flicked it away.  And the tree
became one more woven in the wood.

I went on with the winter wrapped around me.
Somehow it warmed.

## The Last of the Light is not the Last of the Light

Sunset like a world's end
at the world's end –
and the long, high-ridged back of the land
lit with a fingerstroke of dull flame.

Flare of reluctant, sullen heat –

a last illumination of what will be lost,
the cost of it reckoned
by the upturned glance
to the fading, farewell smile of light

before everything went tumbling down into the valley,
the lid shut fast

and the darkness settled its nest in my heart.

*

There was a road, my feet upon it,
a few thorny bushes,
the twittering of lost souls.

Somewhere the sound of rushing water, a black
churn of foam with the night folded into it.

I was following my dreamland's crooked backbone
and with each laboured push forward
shed another skin.
The struggle was simply to stay upright.

The moon like a bird came to sing in my skull.

And ahead, two broken stones, guardians at the crossways,
each one inscribed with the letters of my name.

I spoke them.  The password.

*

The climb uphill was slow but measured –

flutterings in the dark, wind-soughs,
glimmerings – voices heard in another room.

There were footprints ahead of me
darkening the frost, and there were rocks
that were taking the shape of creatures
and something was warming their slow blood.

I moved through the ticking of many long seconds.

Then a cry made me look round, a call
shot over the far edge, as a world spread
its fingers across the prone form of the land

and a peacock's feather lifted me up
so that the next step I took lightly

and came to the high ground on a path of bright air.

# Biography

David Calcutt was born and lives in the West Midlands. He has written many plays for both theatre and radio and published several novels and stories for children, as well as four pamphlets of poetry. *The last of the light is not the last of the light* is David Calcutt's first full poetry collection.

# Publications

**Poetry pamphlets:**

Outlaws (Iron Press), Road Kill and Through the Woods (Fair Acre Press), The Old Man in the House of Bone (V. Press).

**Plays:**

Published plays include, Lady Macbeth, Salem, Beowulf, The Terrible Fate of Humpty Dumpty, Tess of the d'Urbervilles, Dracula (Oxford University Press)

Broadcast plays include, Paper Doll, The Bogeyman, The Otherworld Child, The Daughter of the Sea, Walker in the Night, Lady of Flowers and Feathers, Over Sea, Under Stone, The Dark is Rising, The Last of the Mohicans, Fahrenheit 451, The Return of the Native (BBC).

Theatre Productions include, Ruff Moey, The Ballad of Billy Earp (Theatre Foundry), The Map of Marvels (Pentabus), Assassin of the Sun (Tabard Theatre), Lady Chatterley's Lover, Prospero's Island, The Mothers, The White Shining Land, The Ward, Descent, (Midland Actors Theatre), The Life and Times of the Tat Man, Winter Tales, The Darlaston Dog Fight (Regional Voice Theatre).

**Novels and Stories:**

Crowboy, Shadow Bringer, The Map of Marvels, Why the Sea is Salty, The Journey of Odysseus (Oxford University Press), Robin Hood (Barefoot Books).

## On 'Road Kill'

"There is a constant celebration of the seasons and cycles of the life of the countryside. The holistic, biocentric vision widens in the later poems to embrace folklore and mythology. All this in a luminous accessible verse."
**Keith Sagar** – *Biographer of Ted Hughes, author of Literature and the Crimes against Nature.*

"I am hugely impressed. By concentrating on the small things, really looking at them, Nadia Kingsley and David Calcutt have managed to articulate something enormous. There is something shamanic, redemptive even, about the progress of the poems into the woods."
**Katrina Porteous** – *Poet. Historian. Broadcaster.*

## On 'Through the Woods'

"This is a deeply satisfying, layered work that will bear re-reading."
**Jan Fortune**, *Envoi magazine.*

# On 'The Old Man in the House of Bone'

"The Old Man in the House of Bone is a fable, a fairytale, is a humane and tender account of an old man's mental and physical decline into the final silence.  David Calcutt's imagery grows from the page and fixes itself inside the skull.  He is a master magician, a seeker of darkness."
**Helen Ivory** - *Poet. Visual Artist. Editor of Ink, Sweat & Tears.*

"Having been a nurse on psycho-geriatric wards everything here rang true. This is the best description of the process of dementia I've come across."
**Sam Smith** - *Poet. Author. Editor of The Journal.*

"This precise and striking series of poems is both consequential and sequential; each one building on the previous and the following like sediment, creating a brooding and disquieting atmosphere. Calcutt's poetry is alert and surefooted – written with a humane touch, and always compelling."
 **Jane Commane** - *Poet. Editor/Director of Nine Arches Press.*

# Acknowledgements

Some of the poems in this collection first appeared, some in slightly different forms, in the following publications:

Abridged
Atrium
Bare Fiction
The Cannon's Mouth
Envoi
Ink, Sweat and Tears
Pentameter
Road Kill, pamphlet, Fair Acre Press
Under the Radar
We're All in it Together, anthology, Offa's Press

First published in Great Britain in 2018 by Fair Acre Press
www.fairacrepress.co.uk

Copyright © David Calcutt 2018

A CIP catalogue record for this book is available from the British Library

ISBN  978-1-911048-30-5

Printed and bound by Lightning Source
Lightning Source has received Chain of Custody (CoC) certification
from:
The Forest Stewardship CouncilTM (FSC®)
Programme for the Endorsement of Forest CertificationTM (PEFCTM) The Sustainable
Forestry Initiative® (SFI®).

Vector graphics on the cover created by Kjpargeter - Freepik.com

Typeset by Nadia Kingsley

Cover design by Algimantas Murza

Lightning Source UK Ltd.
Milton Keynes UK
UKHW05f0443090518
322327UK00009B/43/P